I'm All Grown Now, Papa

WRITTEN BY
Claude Louis, MD

ILLUSTRATED BY
Junior Michel

Title: I'm All Grown Now, Papa
Type: Picture book manuscript
Word count: 785
Category: Nonfiction
Age range: 5–9 years old

First published in 2021

Written by Claude Louis, MD
Illustrated by Junior Michel

ISBN: 978-1-7378954-0-4 (hardcover)
ISBN: 978-1-7378954-1-1 (paperback)
ISBN: 978-1-7378954-2-8 (ebook)

Dedication

In memory of Grann (Saintinat Laurensaint)
and my dad Leon Louis. For my brother
Gabriel, my mother and sister.

For my family.

For Melita and Manithe
who fed me when I was hungry
and away from my family.

For Dixie Bickel who raised funds for my
medical school tuition; I could not have done it
without your help.

In memory of Drs. Lyonel Guirand and
Samuel K. Roberts. I miss you.

Other titles in this series
(to be published over the next two years)

1- When Kais Met Toussaint (7-11)

2- The Mountain Boy (Middle Grade)

3- The Girl With The Golden Heart (Early Middle Grade)

You left when I was in rags—
"Just one month old," Grann says.

Now I am big, and I chase my
brother all fifteen kilometers back
home from the market.

My friends sometimes laugh at my smile. My bottom front tooth is pushed back, so it looks like a sunken piano key. Grann says people told you the same, Papa. When I ask about you, Grann says I should just look at myself in the water bucket. We don't have a mirror, but if I look close, I can see my reflection in the water.

I am grown enough to go to school now.
Manman was so excited that she got my
uniform ready a month in advance.
Grann says I will learn **amazing
things** at school.

I take care of Grann and Manman. Grann has taught me to use her **herbal remedies** when someone is sick.

At night, my brother Gabriel and I study by the **gentle light of candles**.

Gabriel's eyes water from the smoke.

Some nights our stomachs growl. We may not always have enough to eat, but we are strong anyway.

Gabriel and I carry the
vegetables to the market,
so we wake up long before the rooster crows.
We sell those vegetables to pay for school.
Manman says it is the only way, Papa.

Both Manman and Grann say that,
since you are gone, Papa, we are
the men of the house.
We do all of your chores.
Papa, I am all grown now.

Gabriel and I
race to school
every day. When we reach
the steep hill, we keep
our heads down and walk
steadily to the very top.

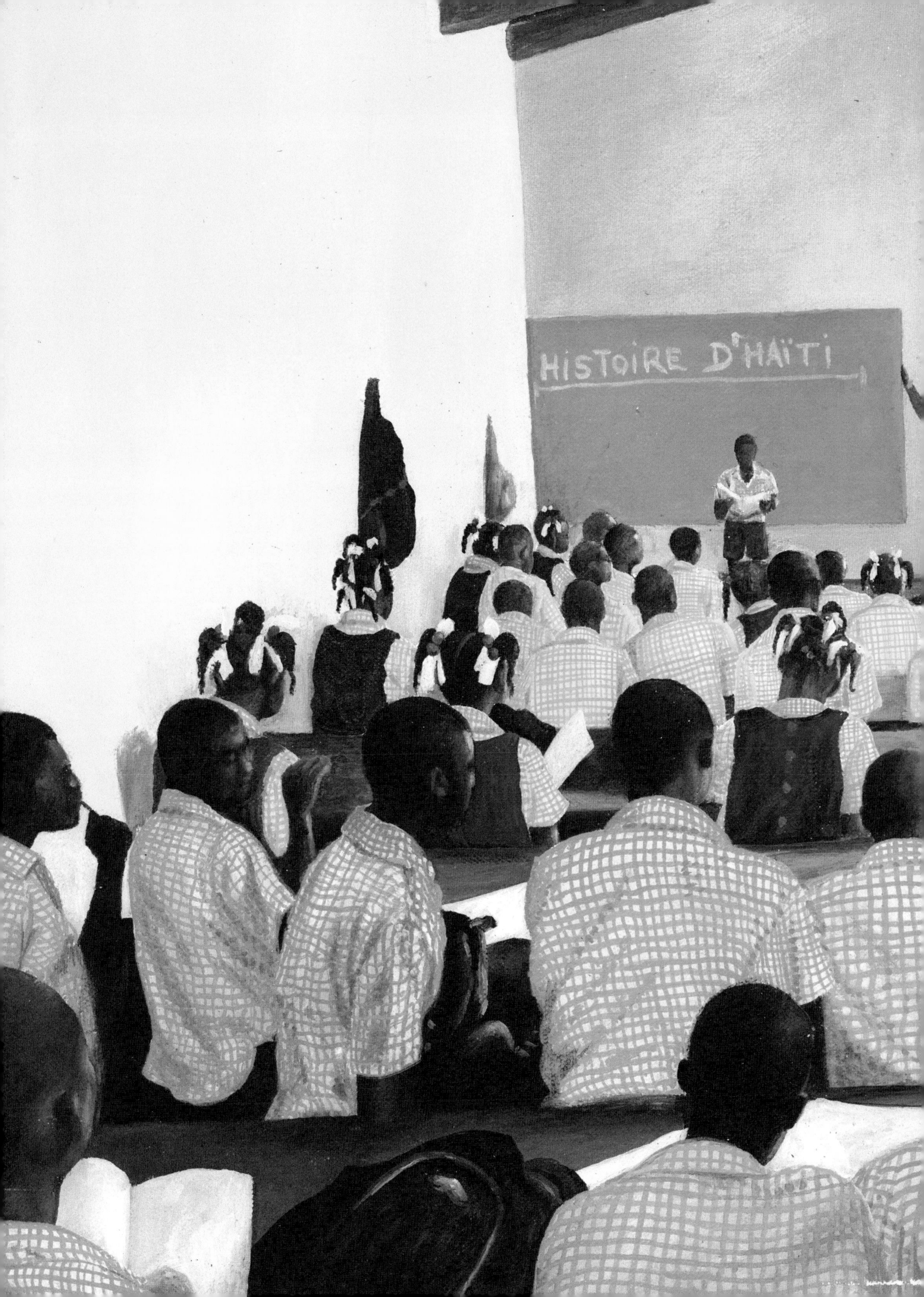
HISTOIRE D'HAÏTI

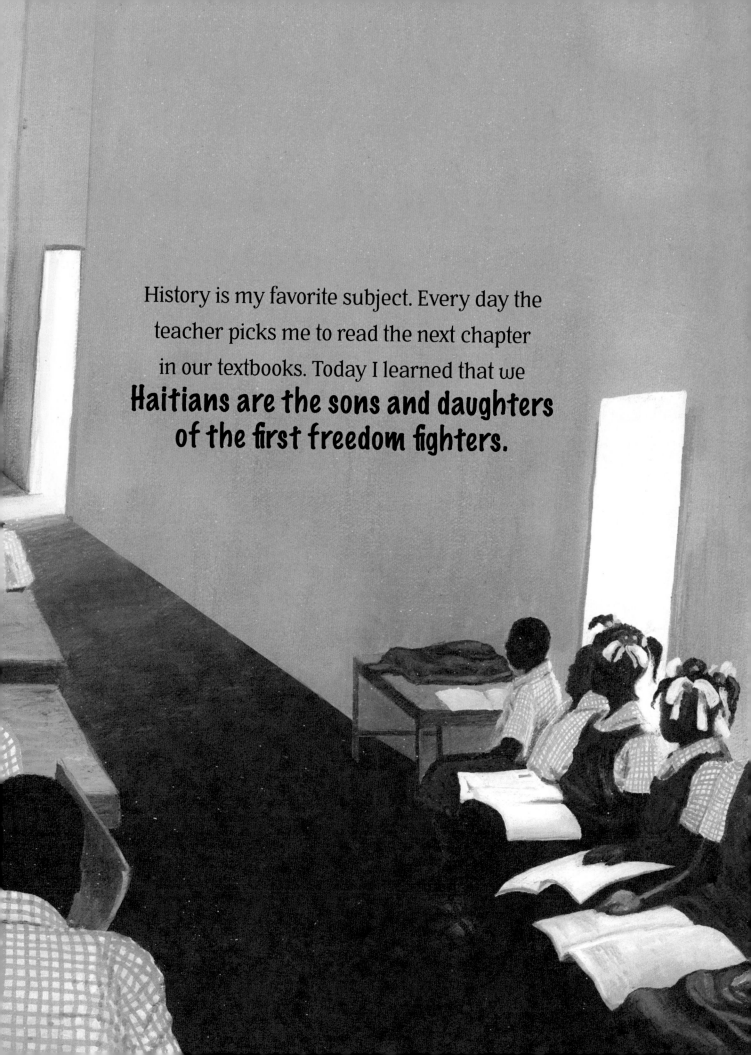

History is my favorite subject. Every day the teacher picks me to read the next chapter in our textbooks. Today I learned that we **Haitians are the sons and daughters of the first freedom fighters.**

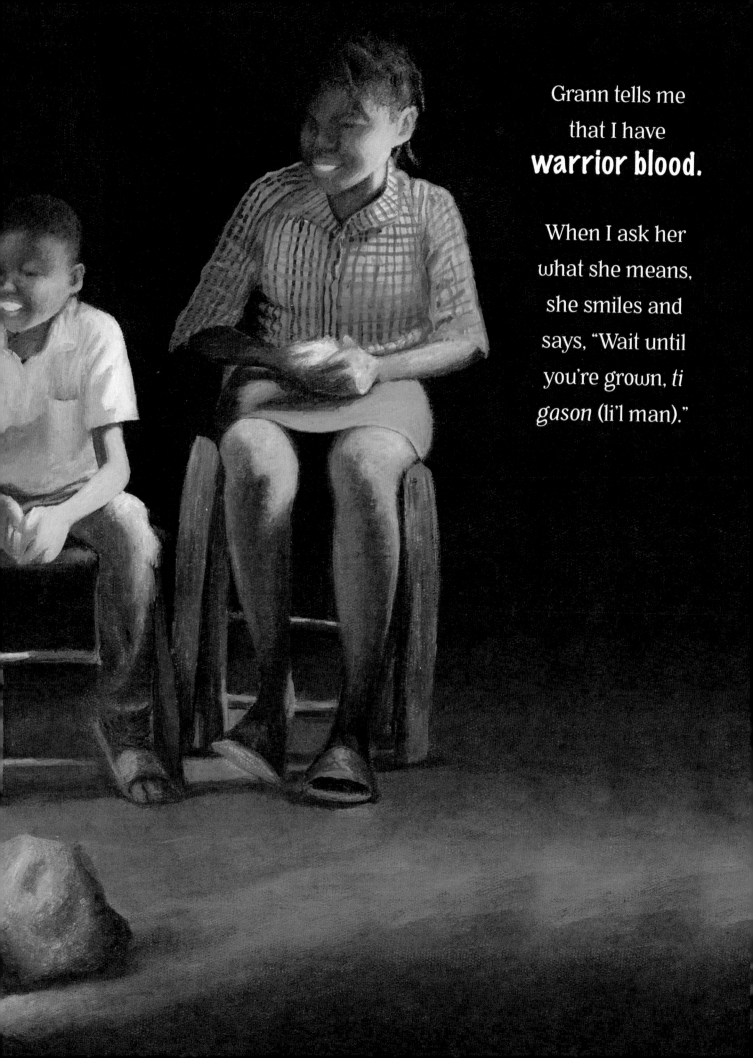

Grann tells me that I have **warrior blood.**

When I ask her what she means, she smiles and says, "Wait until you're grown, *ti gason* (li'l man)."

The other night, Grann told me that I have a
big heart, just like you Papa. A boy I know
at school has a large heart, but he says this
makes him tired and easily winded. I walk fifteen
kilometers with vegetables on my head, and then
run the same distance back home. I never feel
winded, even with my big heart.

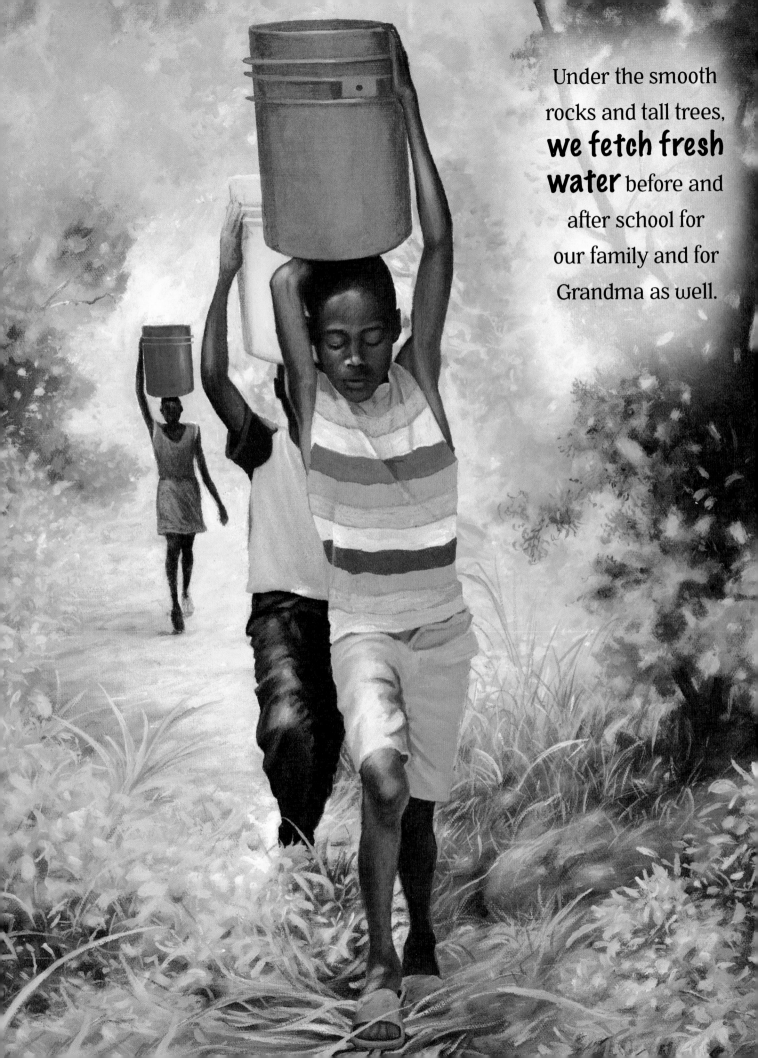

Under the smooth rocks and tall trees, **we fetch fresh water** before and after school for our family and for Grandma as well.

On the mountains, our morning showers before school start with **a jumping warm-up routine**. As soon as the first scoop of freezing water touches my skin, my whole body becomes numb. Sometimes to overcome the panic, we take a few deep breaths, then roar like two lion cubs and at once hit each other with the first splash.

We laugh and sing until we're done.

On weekends, we help Manman
on the farm with the other men she hires.
At least we did before she remarried.

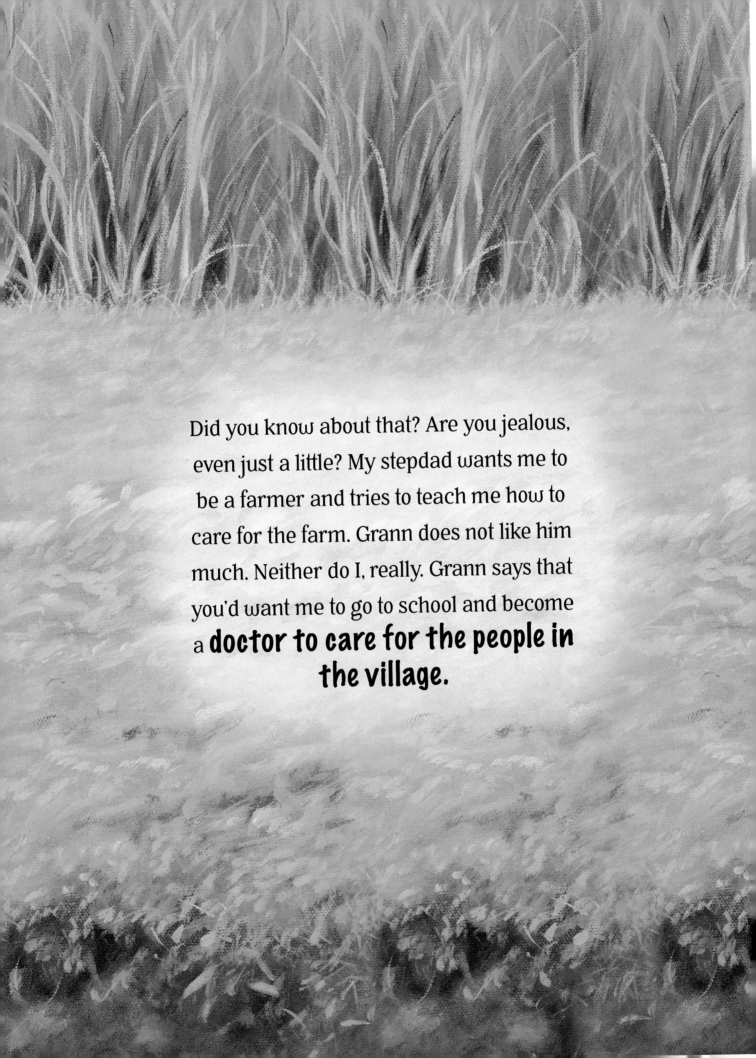

Did you know about that? Are you jealous, even just a little? My stepdad wants me to be a farmer and tries to teach me how to care for the farm. Grann does not like him much. Neither do I, really. Grann says that you'd want me to go to school and become a **doctor to care for the people in the village.**

We still cut down trees, Papa. Now there are barely any left. It makes me sad to see them fall, but it's the only way Manman **can cook for us.** How do you prepare your meals? Do people eat in heaven?

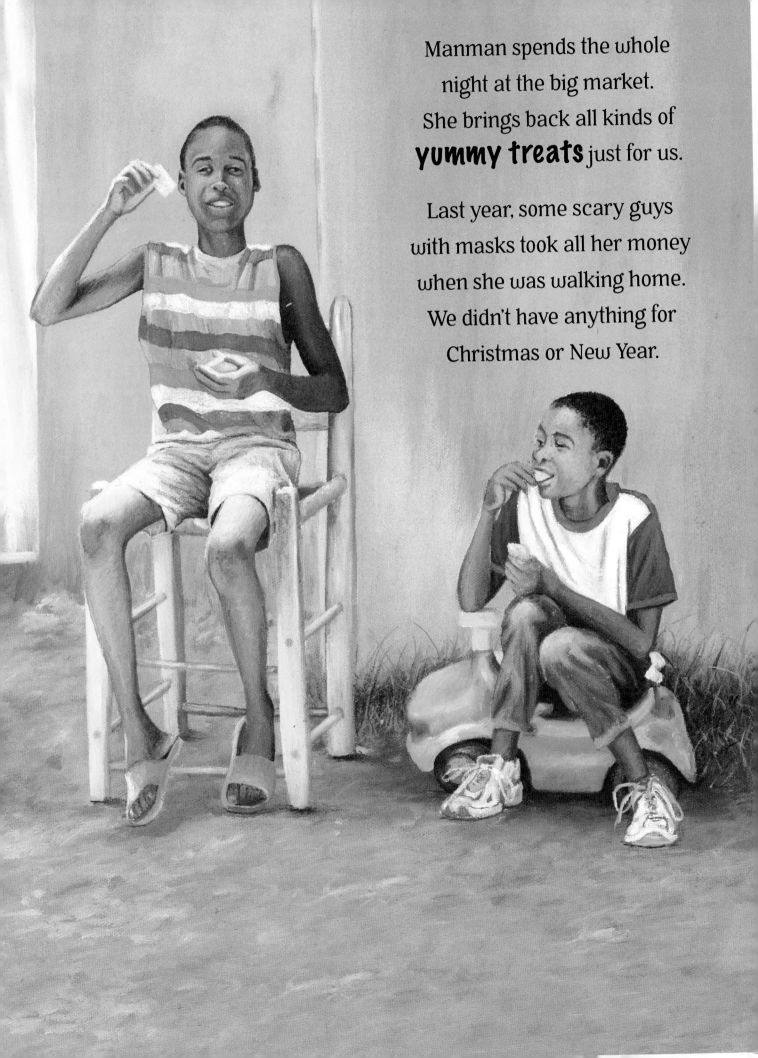

Manman spends the whole night at the big market. She brings back all kinds of **yummy treats** just for us.

Last year, some scary guys with masks took all her money when she was walking home. We didn't have anything for Christmas or New Year.

I never get in trouble because I always do what I'm told and only play after I **finish all my chores.**

Do you work up there? Do you have any friends with you? What is heaven like?

In class, the smell of the fried patties often distracts me from my work. During recess, we eat **sweet sugarcane** for dessert. I like the big stalks, but the woody fibers get stuck in my teeth.

Gabriel and I play
marbles with the
boys of the village.
I like to get the
big blue ones that
look like a
cat's eye.

Gabriel outgrew our little school in the mountains. Now he travels three long hours to get to his new school. On the way there, he carries a **big book bag** on his back and a load of vegetables on his head.

With these books, I'll learn new things
every day, Papa. I will **keep climbing**
until I reach the very top of the mountains.
I'm all grown now, Papa.

Words to the readers from the author

"You are the exact replica of your father," Grann told me over and over. Dr. Leon, as he was known in the village and its surroundings, only had a 5th-grade level. Still, despite his limited education, he evolved into the healer that the village relied on when they became sick, with the help of a traditional healer (his mother, my Grann). I cannot recall the number of times I was told: "If I'm alive today, it's thanks to God and your father."

So from a very young age, I wanted to be just like my dad even when I had no idea what it would take. In addition, I was frequently reminded that folks like me could not become real doctors – the ones who wear a white coat – not a farm boy from Qui-Croit. Twenty years later, I returned to the village as a medical student organizing mobile clinics. After graduating from medical school, I built the first clinic in the village on the site of my family's house. While other people focused on where I came from and my social status; I concentrated on the one thing I could control, my grades. This is a testimony that dreams actually come true when hard work meets opportunity.

Due to the significant, identifiable needs in health care and education in Qui-Croit and its surrounding area, I started Words In Action Haiti in 2008 to provide people with access to health care and improve educational opportunities. From the time I was growing up and still today, less than 30% of children move on to high school. Not only did it take 3 hours (each way) to walk to the closest high school, it was also too expensive for most parents to afford. The result was that very bright children gave up on their dream of getting an education. To access health care, elderly and weakened patients sometimes walk for 5 hours before reaching our clinic.

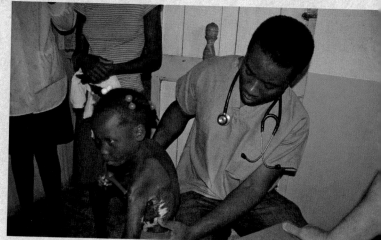

Met Natacha when she was 8. Had life-threatening complications from burn. WIA sponsored her to Shriners in Boston. Had multiple surgeries. Now a normal teenager enjoying school.

Instead of perpetually requesting direct donations for our education projects in Haiti, I wanted to share my story of growing up in the mountains, the struggle and the resilience of Haitians with the world, and in turn, invest all proceeds into the community. Three other children's books are ready to be published, which we hope will be released within the next two years (by 2023). 100% of the profit from these books will go towards educational areas

Patients in the waiting area at Words In Action Community Clinic (2018).

tuition sponsorship, teacher training, library development, and building schools Haiti, starting with the school I attended as a child. Through our foundation, as of early 2021, six students have received a full scholarship for university with the goal of returning to the community as teachers and nurses. Based on our admission and requirements data, there will be at least 2 university students for the academic year 2021-2022. Over 100 children will be sponsored through primary and high school this year. Our goal is to support every single child to receive an education and encourage and support those with higher aptitude to complete a college degree.

Empowering the children and the youth by promoting education is the only way the next generations will prevail. We need to start building a society based on social justice, fairness, equality, and love of country, which is a precious heritage for which our ancestors have fought so hard for. It should serve all of us, not just a few rich and powerful people.

Myself in front of my former primary school in Qui-Croit school during recess (2013).

Current state of my primary school as of 2021.

2 different plans for the school are being considered:

Visual of the plan for the new building.

People are welcome to donate if that is where their heart leads them. To do so, or for more information on ongoing projects, I invite you to visit www.wiahaiti.org and our FaceBook page Words In Action Haiti/Facebook

About the Illustrator

Junior lives in Petion-Ville, Haiti. He started to draw at a very young age. He grew up and continued to learn from his older brother who was an artist. After his studies, he became very well known in the artistic world which has allowed him to take part in many art expositions locally in Haiti at the Festival of Arts Gallery but also at an international level. His work has been shown in France, US, Italy and South Korea.

About the Author

Claude Louis lives in Virginia with his wife and 3 children. He is the founder of Words In Action Haiti, a 501c(3) organization that runs a community clinic and a school sponsorship program in Qui-Croit, Haiti. He returns to Haiti three to four times annually to care for patients, and provides telemedicine support to the on-site nurse. Dr Louis's parallel passion is to help the children of his village receive a better education than he did, to empower the next generation of leaders that will invest their knowledge to uplift their community and country.